Nature of Science • Biological World • Chemical World • Physical World • Earth and Space

Catalyst

Junior Cycle Science

Portfolio

Your companion for change to the new course

Name: ....

Class: ....

School: ....

Patrick Dundon
David King
Maria Sheehan

educate.ie

PUBLISHED BY:
Educate.ie
Walsh Educational Books Ltd
Castleisland, Co. Kerry, Ireland
www.educate.ie

EDITOR:
Julie Steenson

DESIGN AND LAYOUT:
Kieran O'Donoghue

PRINTED AND BOUND BY:
Walsh Colour Print, Castleisland

PHOTOGRAPHS:
Front-cover photograph: Bigstock

ISBN: 978-1-910468-22-7

Contents

Introduction

Welcome to your *Catalyst* portfolio, where you can build up a collection of your Junior Cycle Science work and store it safely.

Using this portfolio, you can:

- Write up the steps and results of your Scientific Investigations.
- Record your research and findings for Science in Society tasks.
- Evaluate what you have learned at the end of each chapter.
- Reflect on the end-of-chapter Big Challenges.

Note that what you record in these pages may differ depending on the task you are undertaking, so it may not always be necessary to complete every section on a page.

This portfolio is also available on educateplus.ie.

Have fun completing the tasks!

Patrick Dundon, David King and Maria Sheehan, 2016

Key Skills

Working on key skills is an important part of your development as a student, and as a person. You should keep the following skills in mind during every scientific task and record the skills you have developed when the task is complete:

- Managing myself
- Being creative
- Managing information and thinking
- Working with others
- Staying well
- Communicating
- Being literate
- Being numerate

Scientific Investigations

Scientific Investigation

Title: ....

Nature of Science ☐

Biological World ☐

Chemical World ☐

Physical World ☐

Earth and Space ☐

Chapter number: ....

Page number: ....

Date: ....

Lab partner(s): ....

....

1. Introduction to investigation and background information

Hypothesis

2. Investigation design

Variables

a. Independent variable

b. Dependent variable

c. Controlled (fixed) variables

d. Control (if necessary)

Equipment

Method

Labelled diagram

Safety

3. Investigation results

a. Obtaining and recording data

Table

b. Presenting data

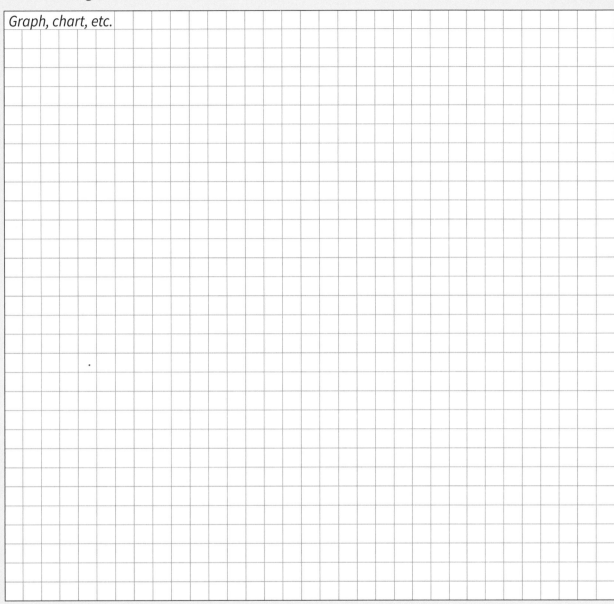

Graph, chart, etc.

c. Analysing data

Calculations, trends, etc.

4. Investigation evaluation

5. Investigation conclusion

6. References

7. Key skills development

Key skills	How I developed these skills during this task

Scientific Investigation

Title:..

Nature of Science	☐	Chapter number:..
Biological World	☐	Page number:..
Chemical World	☐	Date: ....
Physical World	☐	Lab partner(s):...
Earth and Space	☐	....

1. Introduction to investigation and background information

____

____

____

Hypothesis

____

____

2. Investigation design

Variables

a. Independent variable

____

b. Dependent variable

____

c. Controlled (fixed) variables

____

d. Control (if necessary)

____

Equipment

____

____

Method

Labelled diagram

Safety

3. Investigation results

a. Obtaining and recording data

Table

b. Presenting data

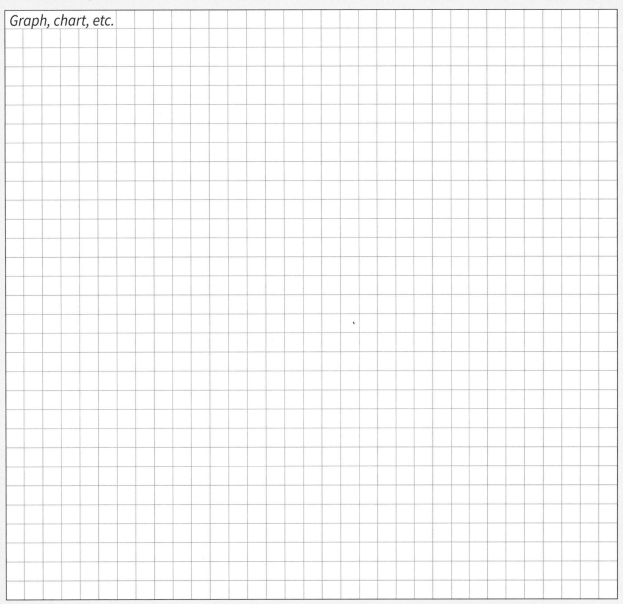

Graph, chart, etc.

c. Analysing data

Calculations, trends, etc.

4. Investigation evaluation

5. Investigation conclusion

6. References

7. Key skills development

Key skills	How I developed these skills during this task

Scientific Investigation

Title: ....

Nature of Science ☐

Biological World ☐

Chemical World ☐

Physical World ☐

Earth and Space ☐

Chapter number: ....

Page number: ....

Date: ....

Lab partner(s): ....

....

1. Introduction to investigation and background information

Hypothesis

2. Investigation design

Variables

a. Independent variable

b. Dependent variable

c. Controlled (fixed) variables

d. Control (if necessary)

Equipment

Method

Labelled diagram

Safety

3. Investigation results

a. Obtaining and recording data

Table

b. Presenting data

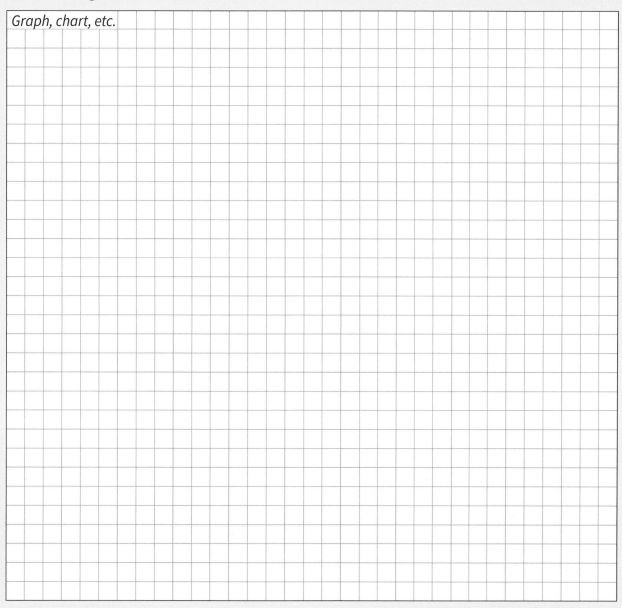

Graph, chart, etc.

c. Analysing data

Calculations, trends, etc.

4. Investigation evaluation

5. Investigation conclusion

6. References

7. Key skills development

Key skills	How I developed these skills during this task

Scientific Investigation

Title: ....

Nature of Science ☐
Biological World ☐
Chemical World ☐
Physical World ☐
Earth and Space ☐

Chapter number: ....
Page number: ....
Date: ....
Lab partner(s): ....
....

1. Introduction to investigation and background information

Hypothesis

---

2. Investigation design

Variables

a. Independent variable

---

b. Dependent variable

---

c. Controlled (fixed) variables

---

d. Control (if necessary)

Equipment

Method

Labelled diagram

Safety

3. Investigation results

a. Obtaining and recording data

Table

b. Presenting data

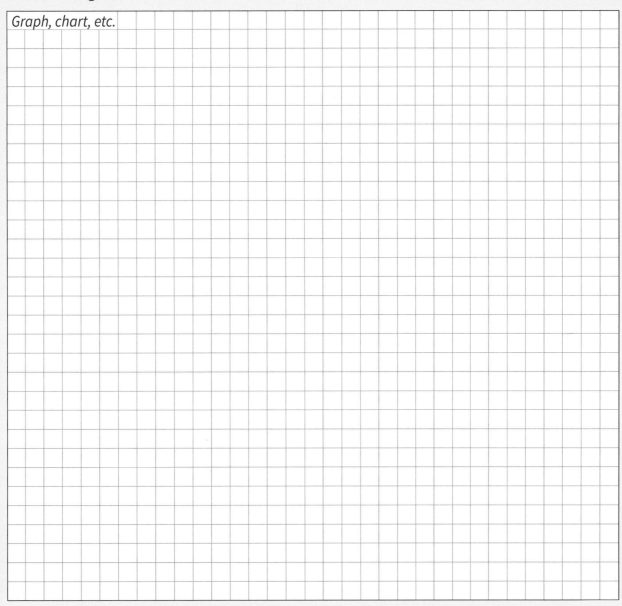

Graph, chart, etc.

c. Analysing data

Calculations, trends, etc.

4. Investigation evaluation

5. Investigation conclusion

6. References

7. Key skills development

Key skills	How I developed these skills during this task

Scientific Investigation

Title: ....

Nature of Science	☐	Chapter number: ....
Biological World	☐	Page number: ....
Chemical World	☐	Date: ....
Physical World	☐	Lab partner(s): ....
Earth and Space	☐	....

1. Introduction to investigation and background information

____

____

____

Hypothesis

____

____

2. Investigation design

Variables

a. Independent variable

____

b. Dependent variable

____

c. Controlled (fixed) variables

____

d. Control (if necessary)

____

Equipment

____

____

Method

Labelled diagram

Safety

3. Investigation results

a. Obtaining and recording data

Table

b. Presenting data

Graph, chart, etc.

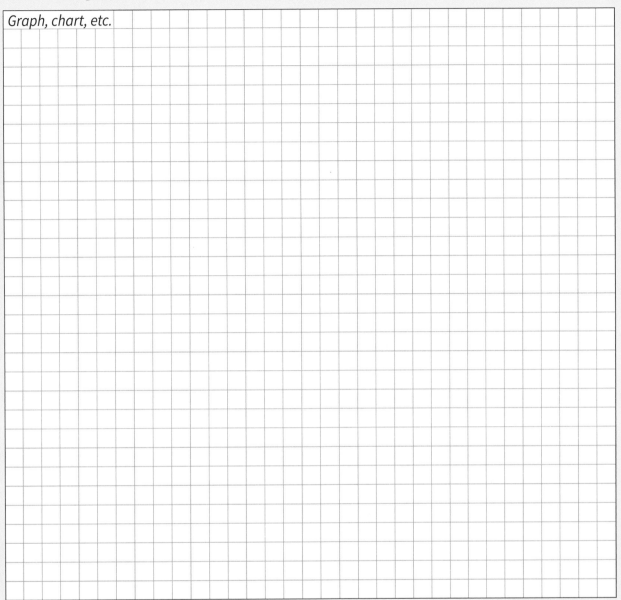

c. Analysing data

Calculations, trends, etc.

4. Investigation evaluation

5. Investigation conclusion

6. References

7. Key skills development

Key skills	How I developed these skills during this task

Scientific Investigation

Title: ....

Nature of Science ☐

Biological World ☐

Chemical World ☐

Physical World ☐

Earth and Space ☐

Chapter number: ....

Page number: ....

Date: ....

Lab partner(s): ....

....

1. Introduction to investigation and background information

____

____

____

Hypothesis

____

____

2. Investigation design

Variables

a. Independent variable

____

b. Dependent variable

____

c. Controlled (fixed) variables

____

d. Control (if necessary)

____

Equipment

____

____

Method

Labelled diagram

Safety

3. Investigation results

a. Obtaining and recording data

Table

b. Presenting data

Graph, chart, etc.

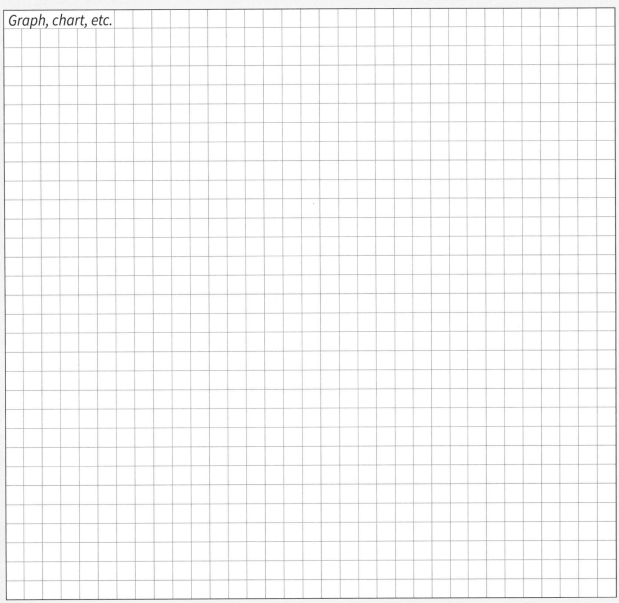

c. Analysing data

Calculations, trends, etc.

4. Investigation evaluation

5. Investigation conclusion

6. References

7. Key skills development

Key skills	How I developed these skills during this task

Scientific Investigation

Title: ....

Nature of Science ☐
Biological World ☐
Chemical World ☐
Physical World ☐
Earth and Space ☐

Chapter number: ....

Page number: ....

Date: ....

Lab partner(s): ....

....

1. Introduction to investigation and background information

____

____

____

Hypothesis

____

____

2. Investigation design

Variables

a. Independent variable

____

b. Dependent variable

____

c. Controlled (fixed) variables

____

d. Control (if necessary)

____

Equipment

____

____

Method

Labelled diagram

Safety

3. Investigation results

a. Obtaining and recording data

Table

b. Presenting data

Graph, chart, etc.

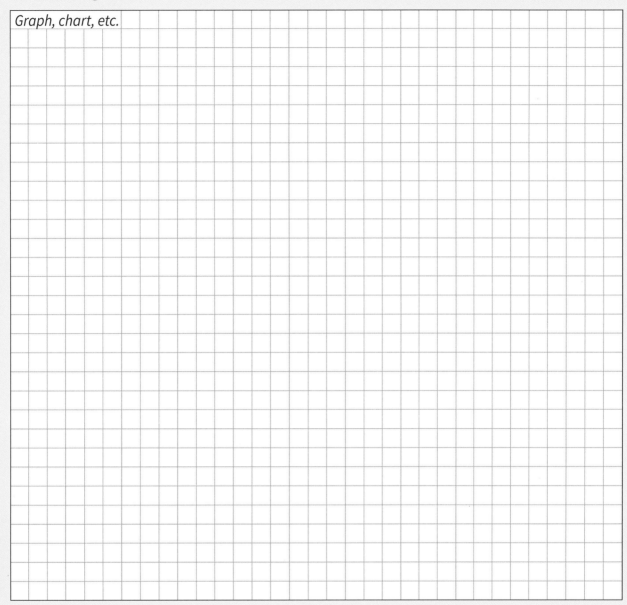

c. Analysing data

Calculations, trends, etc.

4. Investigation evaluation

5. Investigation conclusion

6. References

7. Key skills development

Key skills	How I developed these skills during this task

Scientific Investigation

Title: ....

Nature of Science ☐

Biological World ☐

Chemical World ☐

Physical World ☐

Earth and Space ☐

Chapter number: ....

Page number: ....

Date: ....

Lab partner(s): ....

....

1. Introduction to investigation and background information

____

____

____

Hypothesis

____

____

2. Investigation design

Variables

a. Independent variable

____

b. Dependent variable

____

c. Controlled (fixed) variables

____

d. Control (if necessary)

____

Equipment

____

____

Method

Labelled diagram

Safety

3. Investigation results

a. Obtaining and recording data

Table

b. Presenting data

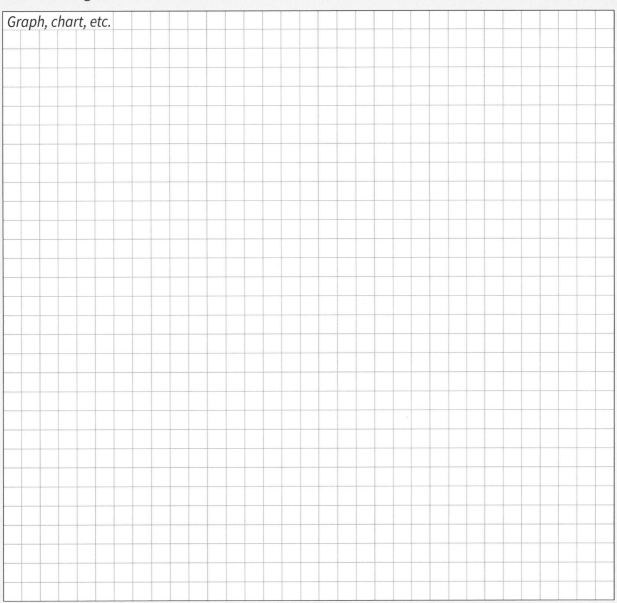

Graph, chart, etc.

c. Analysing data

Calculations, trends, etc.

4. Investigation evaluation

5. Investigation conclusion

6. References

7. Key skills development

Key skills	How I developed these skills during this task

Scientific Investigation

Title: ....

Nature of Science	☐	Chapter number: ....
Biological World	☐	Page number: ....
Chemical World	☐	Date: ....
Physical World	☐	Lab partner(s): ....
Earth and Space	☐	....

1. Introduction to investigation and background information

___

___

___

Hypothesis

___

___

2. Investigation design

Variables

a. Independent variable

___

b. Dependent variable

___

c. Controlled (fixed) variables

___

d. Control (if necessary)

___

Equipment

___

___

Method

Labelled diagram

Safety

3. Investigation results

a. Obtaining and recording data

Table

b. Presenting data

Graph, chart, etc.

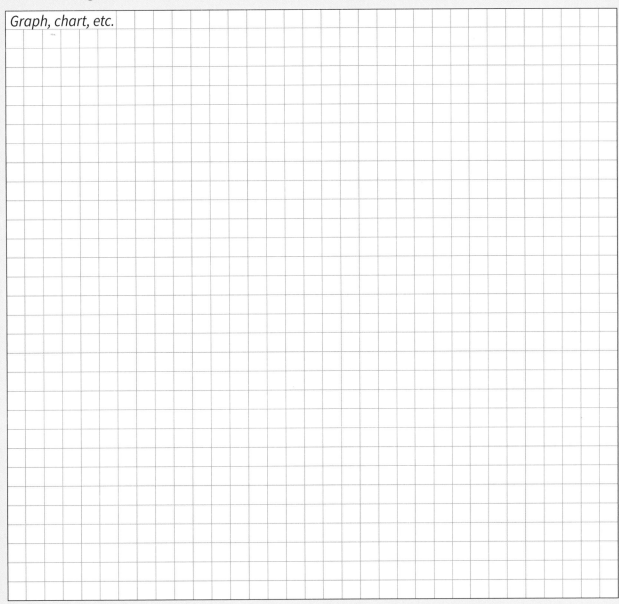

c. Analysing data

Calculations, trends, etc.

4. Investigation evaluation

5. Investigation conclusion

6. References

7. Key skills development

Key skills	How I developed these skills during this task

Scientific Investigation

Title: ....

Nature of Science ☐

Biological World ☐

Chemical World ☐

Physical World ☐

Earth and Space ☐

Chapter number: ....

Page number: ....

Date: ....

Lab partner(s): ....

....

1. Introduction to investigation and background information

___

___

___

Hypothesis

___

___

2. Investigation design

Variables

a. Independent variable

___

b. Dependent variable

___

c. Controlled (fixed) variables

___

d. Control (if necessary)

___

Equipment

___

___

Method

Labelled diagram

Safety

3. Investigation results

a. Obtaining and recording data

Table

b. Presenting data

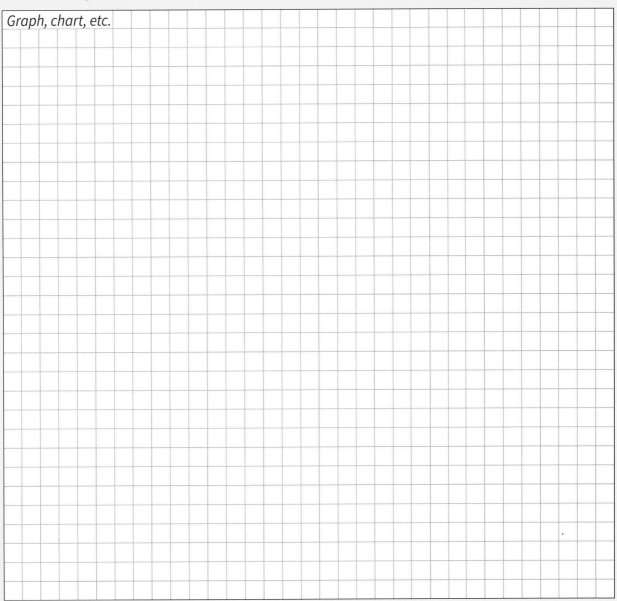

Graph, chart, etc.

c. Analysing data

Calculations, trends, etc.

4. Investigation evaluation

5. Investigation conclusion

6. References

7. Key skills development

Key skills	How I developed these skills during this task

Scientific Investigation

Title:..

Nature of Science	☐	Chapter number:..
Biological World	☐	Page number:..
Chemical World	☐	Date:..
Physical World	☐	Lab partner(s):..
Earth and Space	☐	....

1. Introduction to investigation and background information

___

___

___

Hypothesis

___

___

2. Investigation design

Variables

a. Independent variable

___

b. Dependent variable

___

c. Controlled (fixed) variables

___

d. Control (if necessary)

___

Equipment

___

___

Method

Labelled diagram

Safety

3. Investigation results

a. Obtaining and recording data

Table

b. Presenting data

Graph, chart, etc.

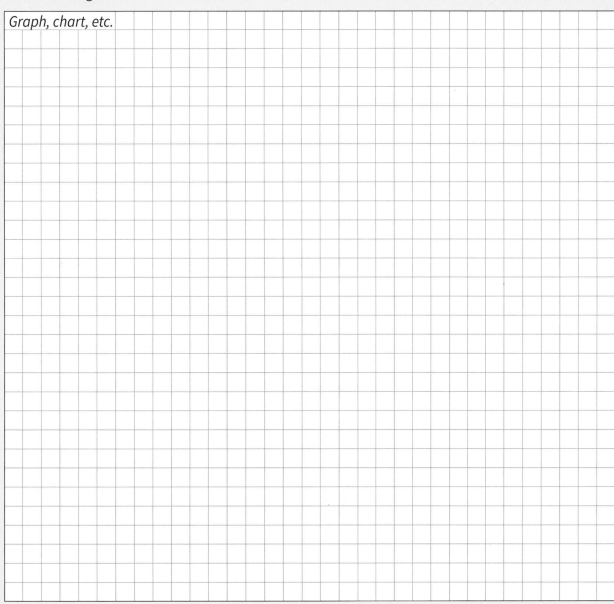

c. Analysing data

Calculations, trends, etc.

4. Investigation evaluation

5. Investigation conclusion

6. References

7. Key skills development

Key skills	How I developed these skills during this task

Scientific Investigation

Title: ....

Nature of Science ☐
Biological World ☐
Chemical World ☐
Physical World ☐
Earth and Space ☐

Chapter number: ....

Page number: ....

Date: ....

Lab partner(s): ....

....

1. Introduction to investigation and background information

____

____

____

Hypothesis

____

____

2. Investigation design

Variables

a. Independent variable

____

b. Dependent variable

____

c. Controlled (fixed) variables

____

d. Control (if necessary)

____

Equipment

____

____

Method

Labelled diagram

Safety

3. Investigation results

a. Obtaining and recording data

Table

b. Presenting data

Graph, chart, etc.

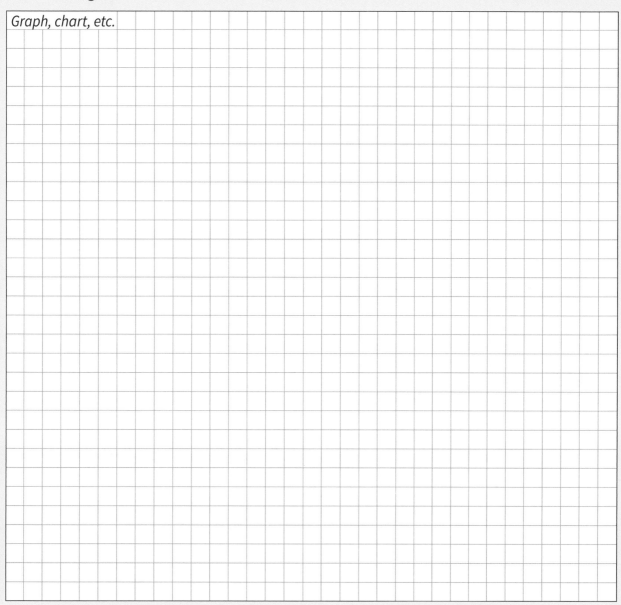

c. Analysing data

Calculations, trends, etc.

4. Investigation evaluation

5. Investigation conclusion

6. References

7. Key skills development

Key skills	How I developed these skills during this task

Scientific Investigation

Title: ....

Nature of Science ☐

Biological World ☐

Chemical World ☐

Physical World ☐

Earth and Space ☐

Chapter number: ....

Page number: ....

Date: ....

Lab partner(s): ....

....

1. Introduction to investigation and background information

Hypothesis

2. Investigation design

Variables

a. Independent variable

b. Dependent variable

c. Controlled (fixed) variables

d. Control (if necessary)

Equipment

Method

Labelled diagram

Safety

3. Investigation results

a. Obtaining and recording data

Table

b. Presenting data

Graph, chart, etc.

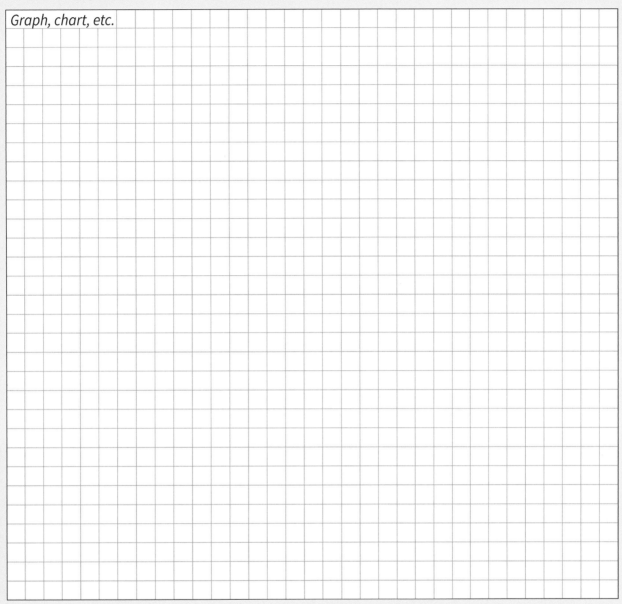

c. Analysing data

Calculations, trends, etc.

4. Investigation evaluation

5. Investigation conclusion

6. References

7. Key skills development

Key skills	How I developed these skills during this task

Scientific Investigation

Title: ....

Nature of Science ☐

Biological World ☐

Chemical World ☐

Physical World ☐

Earth and Space ☐

Chapter number: ....

Page number: ....

Date: ....

Lab partner(s): ....

....

1. Introduction to investigation and background information

___

___

___

Hypothesis

___

___

2. Investigation design

Variables

a. Independent variable

___

b. Dependent variable

___

c. Controlled (fixed) variables

___

d. Control (if necessary)

___

Equipment

___

___

Method

Labelled diagram

Safety

3. Investigation results

a. Obtaining and recording data

Table

b. Presenting data

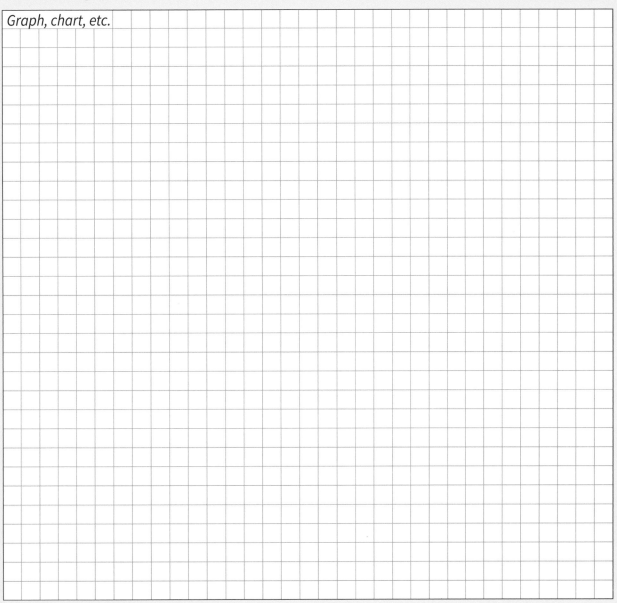

Graph, chart, etc.

c. Analysing data

Calculations, trends, etc.

4. Investigation evaluation

5. Investigation conclusion

6. References

7. Key skills development

Key skills	How I developed these skills during this task

Scientific Investigation

Title: ....

Nature of Science	☐	Chapter number: ....
Biological World	☐	Page number: ....
Chemical World	☐	Date: ....
Physical World	☐	Lab partner(s): ....
Earth and Space	☐	....

1. Introduction to investigation and background information

Hypothesis

2. Investigation design

Variables

a. Independent variable

b. Dependent variable

c. Controlled (fixed) variables

d. Control (if necessary)

Equipment

Method

Labelled diagram

Safety

3. Investigation results

a. Obtaining and recording data

Table

b. Presenting data

Graph, chart, etc.

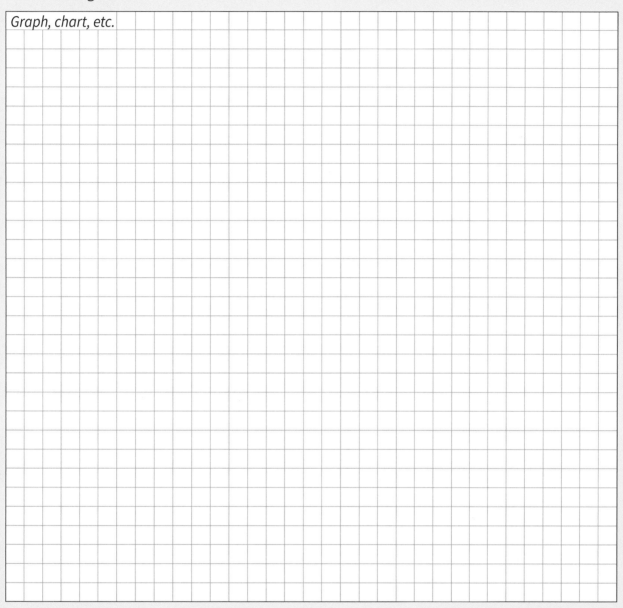

c. Analysing data

Calculations, trends, etc.

4. Investigation evaluation

5. Investigation conclusion

6. References

7. Key skills development

Key skills	How I developed these skills during this task

Scientific Investigation

Title:……………………………………………………

Nature of Science ☐ Biological World ☐ Chemical World ☐ Physical World ☐ Earth and Space ☐

Chapter number:……………………………………………………

Page number:……………………………………………………

Date: ……………………………………………………

Lab partner(s): ……………………………………………………

……………………………………………………

1. Introduction to investigation and background information

___

___

___

Hypothesis

___

___

2. Investigation design

Variables

a. Independent variable

___

b. Dependent variable

___

c. Controlled (fixed) variables

___

d. Control (if necessary)

___

Equipment

___

___

Method

Labelled diagram

Safety

3. Investigation results

a. Obtaining and recording data

Table

b. Presenting data

Graph, chart, etc.

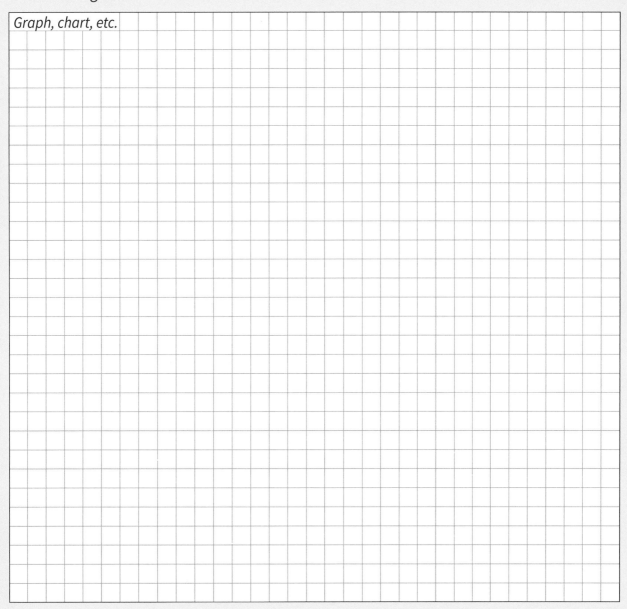

c. Analysing data

Calculations, trends, etc.

4. Investigation evaluation

5. Investigation conclusion

6. References

7. Key skills development

Key skills	How I developed these skills during this task

Scientific Investigation

Title: ....

Nature of Science ☐

Biological World ☐

Chemical World ☐

Physical World ☐

Earth and Space ☐

Chapter number: ....

Page number: ....

Date: ....

Lab partner(s): ....

....

1. Introduction to investigation and background information

____

____

____

Hypothesis

____

____

2. Investigation design

Variables

a. Independent variable

____

b. Dependent variable

____

c. Controlled (fixed) variables

____

d. Control (if necessary)

____

Equipment

____

____

Method

Labelled diagram

Safety

3. Investigation results

a. Obtaining and recording data

Table

b. Presenting data

Graph, chart, etc.

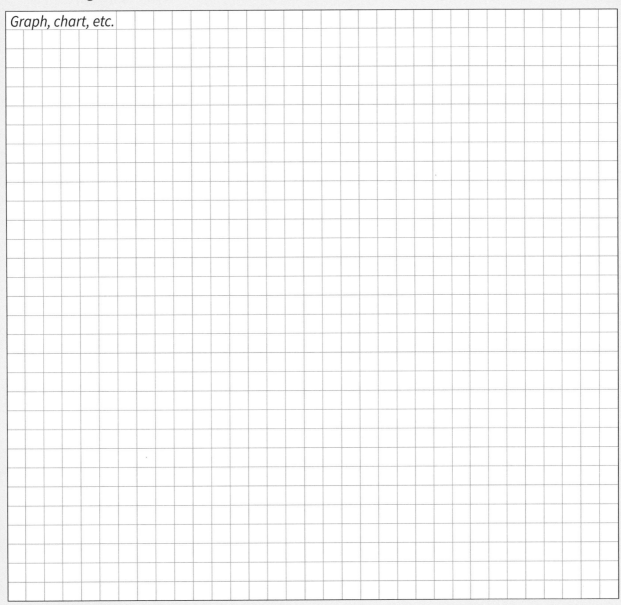

c. Analysing data

Calculations, trends, etc.

4. Investigation evaluation

5. Investigation conclusion

6. References

7. Key skills development

Key skills	How I developed these skills during this task

Scientific Investigation

Title:..

Nature of Science	☐	Chapter number:..
Biological World	☐	Page number:...
Chemical World	☐	Date:..
Physical World	☐	Lab partner(s):..
Earth and Space	☐	....

1. Introduction to investigation and background information

Hypothesis

2. Investigation design

Variables

a. Independent variable

b. Dependent variable

c. Controlled (fixed) variables

d. Control (if necessary)

Equipment

Method

Labelled diagram

Safety

3. Investigation results

a. Obtaining and recording data

Table

b. Presenting data

Graph, chart, etc.

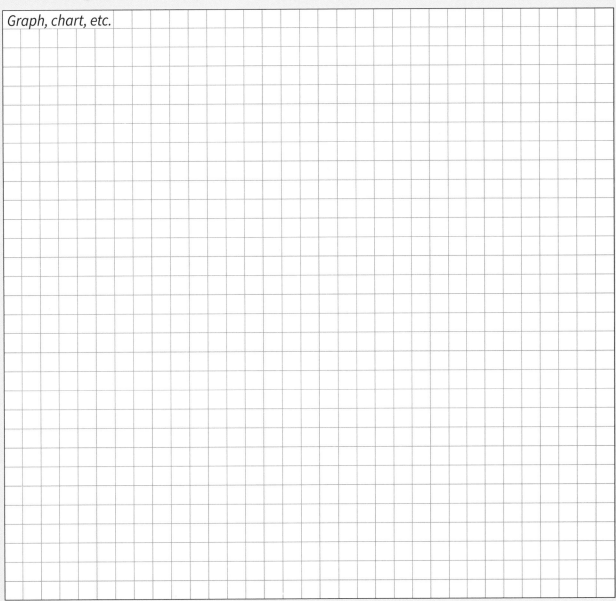

c. Analysing data

Calculations, trends, etc.

4. Investigation evaluation

5. Investigation conclusion

6. References

7. Key skills development

Key skills	How I developed these skills during this task

Scientific Investigation

Title: ....

Nature of Science	☐	Chapter number: ....
Biological World	☐	Page number: ....
Chemical World	☐	Date: ....
Physical World	☐	Lab partner(s): ....
Earth and Space	☐	....

1. Introduction to investigation and background information

Hypothesis

2. Investigation design

Variables

a. Independent variable

b. Dependent variable

c. Controlled (fixed) variables

d. Control (if necessary)

Equipment

Method

Labelled diagram

Safety

3. Investigation results

a. Obtaining and recording data

Table

b. Presenting data

Graph, chart, etc.

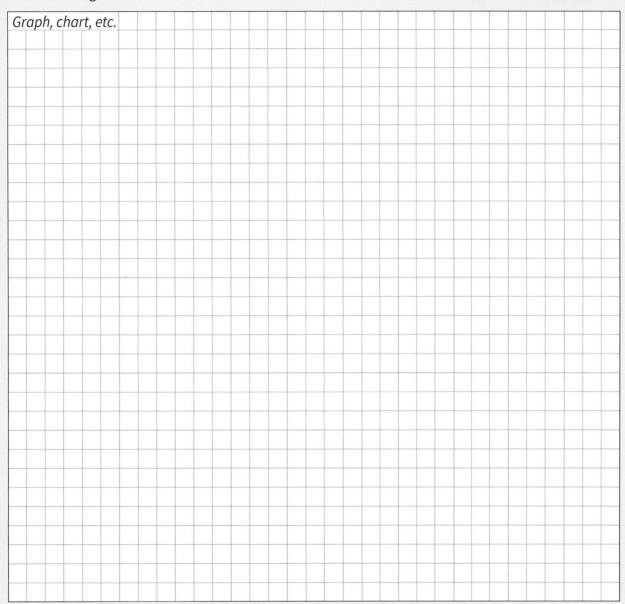

c. Analysing data

Calculations, trends, etc.

4. Investigation evaluation

5. Investigation conclusion

6. References

7. Key skills development

Key skills	How I developed these skills during this task

Scientific Investigation

Title: ....

Nature of Science	☐	Chapter number: ....
Biological World	☐	Page number: ....
Chemical World	☐	Date: ....
Physical World	☐	Lab partner(s): ....
Earth and Space	☐	....

1. Introduction to investigation and background information

___

___

___

Hypothesis

___

___

2. Investigation design

Variables

a. Independent variable

___

b. Dependent variable

___

c. Controlled (fixed) variables

___

d. Control (if necessary)

___

Equipment

___

___

Method

Labelled diagram

Safety

3. Investigation results

a. Obtaining and recording data

Table

b. Presenting data

Graph, chart, etc.

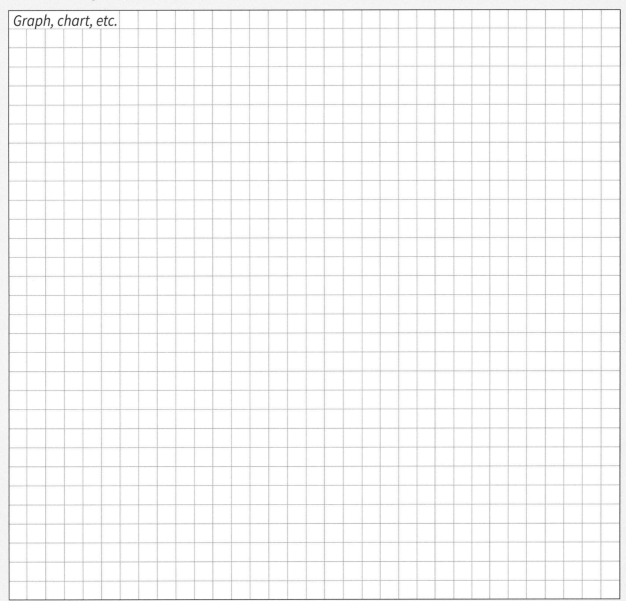

c. Analysing data

Calculations, trends, etc.

4. Investigation evaluation

5. Investigation conclusion

6. References

7. Key skills development

Key skills	How I developed these skills during this task

Scientific Investigation

Title: ....

Nature of Science ☐

Biological World ☐

Chemical World ☐

Physical World ☐

Earth and Space ☐

Chapter number: ....

Page number: ....

Date: ....

Lab partner(s): ....

....

1. Introduction to investigation and background information

Hypothesis

2. Investigation design

Variables

a. Independent variable

b. Dependent variable

c. Controlled (fixed) variables

d. Control (if necessary)

Equipment

Method

Labelled diagram

Safety

3. Investigation results

a. Obtaining and recording data

Table

b. Presenting data

Graph, chart, etc.

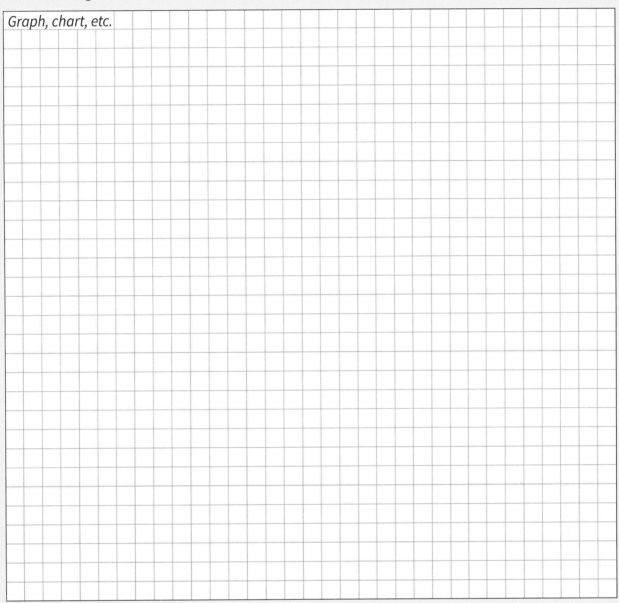

c. Analysing data

Calculations, trends, etc.

4. Investigation evaluation

5. Investigation conclusion

6. References

7. Key skills development

Key skills	How I developed these skills during this task

Scientific Investigation

Title: ....

Nature of Science ☐

Biological World ☐

Chemical World ☐

Physical World ☐

Earth and Space ☐

Chapter number: ....

Page number: ....

Date: ....

Lab partner(s): ....

....

1. Introduction to investigation and background information

___

___

___

Hypothesis

___

___

2. Investigation design

Variables

a. Independent variable

___

b. Dependent variable

___

c. Controlled (fixed) variables

___

d. Control (if necessary)

___

Equipment

___

___

Method

Labelled diagram

Safety

3. Investigation results

a. Obtaining and recording data

Table

b. Presenting data

Graph, chart, etc.

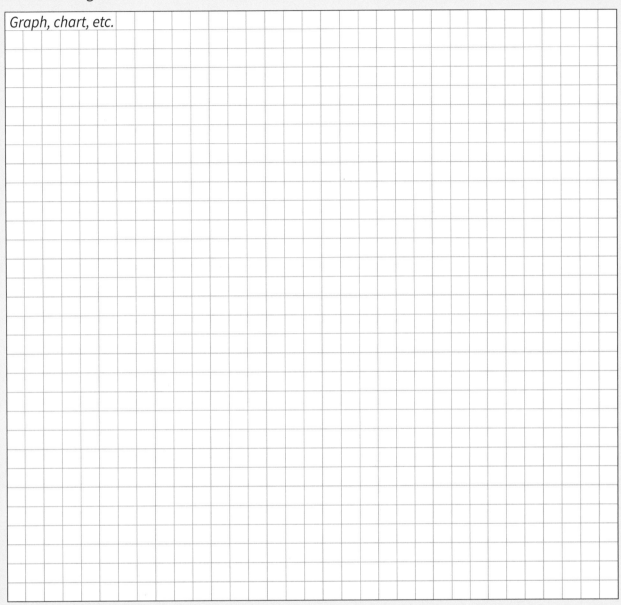

c. Analysing data

Calculations, trends, etc.

4. Investigation evaluation

5. Investigation conclusion

6. References

7. Key skills development

Key skills	How I developed these skills during this task

Scientific Investigation

Title: ....

Nature of Science ☐

Biological World ☐

Chemical World ☐

Physical World ☐

Earth and Space ☐

Chapter number: ....

Page number: ....

Date: ....

Lab partner(s): ....

....

1. Introduction to investigation and background information

Hypothesis

2. Investigation design

Variables

a. Independent variable

b. Dependent variable

c. Controlled (fixed) variables

d. Control (if necessary)

Equipment

Method

Labelled diagram

Safety

3. Investigation results

a. Obtaining and recording data

Table

b. Presenting data

Graph, chart, etc.

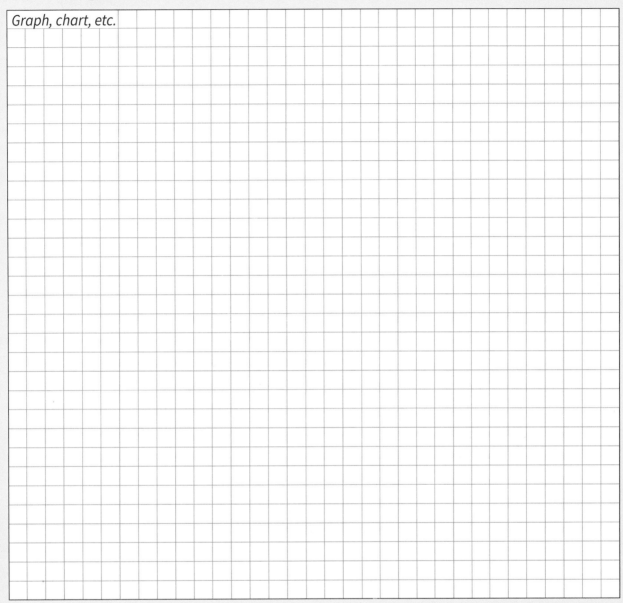

c. Analysing data

Calculations, trends, etc.

4. Investigation evaluation

5. Investigation conclusion

6. References

7. Key skills development

Key skills	How I developed these skills during this task

Scientific Investigation

Title: ....

Nature of Science ☐

Biological World ☐

Chemical World ☐

Physical World ☐

Earth and Space ☐

Chapter number: ....

Page number: ....

Date: ....

Lab partner(s): ....

....

1. Introduction to investigation and background information

____

____

____

Hypothesis

____

____

2. Investigation design

Variables

a. Independent variable

____

b. Dependent variable

____

c. Controlled (fixed) variables

____

d. Control (if necessary)

____

Equipment

____

____

Method

Labelled diagram

Safety

3. Investigation results

a. Obtaining and recording data

Table

b. Presenting data

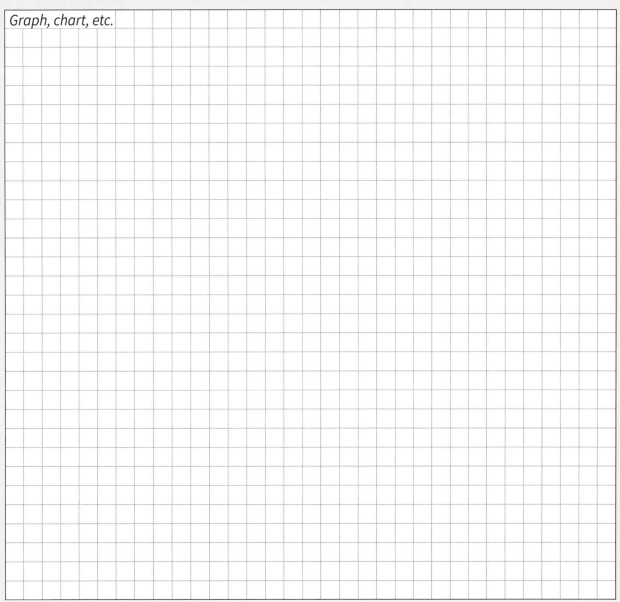

Graph, chart, etc.

c. Analysing data

Calculations, trends, etc.

4. Investigation evaluation

5. Investigation conclusion

6. References

7. Key skills development

Key skills	How I developed these skills during this task

Scientific Investigation

Title: ....

Nature of Science ☐

Biological World ☐

Chemical World ☐

Physical World ☐

Earth and Space ☐

Chapter number: ....

Page number: ....

Date: ....

Lab partner(s): ....

....

1. Introduction to investigation and background information

Hypothesis

2. Investigation design

Variables

a. Independent variable

b. Dependent variable

c. Controlled (fixed) variables

d. Control (if necessary)

Equipment

Method

Labelled diagram

Safety

3. Investigation results

a. Obtaining and recording data

Table

b. Presenting data

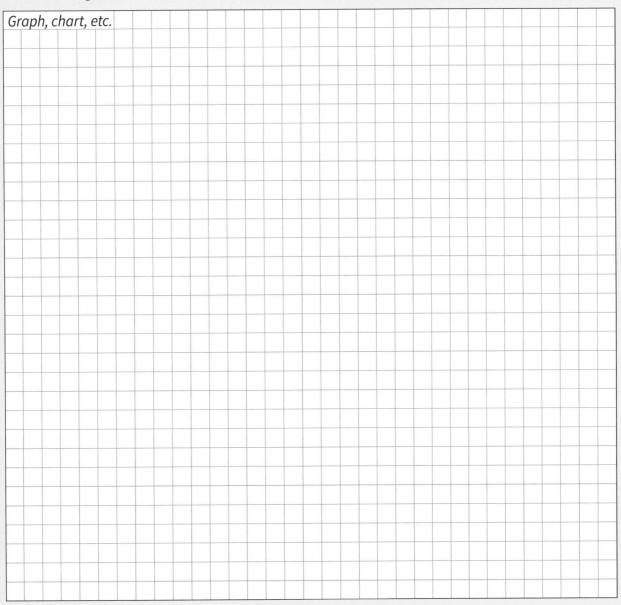

Graph, chart, etc.

c. Analysing data

Calculations, trends, etc.

4. Investigation evaluation

5. Investigation conclusion

6. References

7. Key skills development

Key skills	How I developed these skills during this task

Scientific Investigation

Title: ....

Nature of Science ☐ Chapter number: ....

Biological World ☐ Page number: ....

Chemical World ☐ Date: ....

Physical World ☐ Lab partner(s): ....

Earth and Space ☐ ....

1. Introduction to investigation and background information

____

____

____

Hypothesis

____

____

2. Investigation design

Variables

a. Independent variable

____

b. Dependent variable

____

c. Controlled (fixed) variables

____

d. Control (if necessary)

____

Equipment

____

____

Method

Labelled diagram

Safety

3. Investigation results

a. Obtaining and recording data

Table

b. Presenting data

Graph, chart, etc.

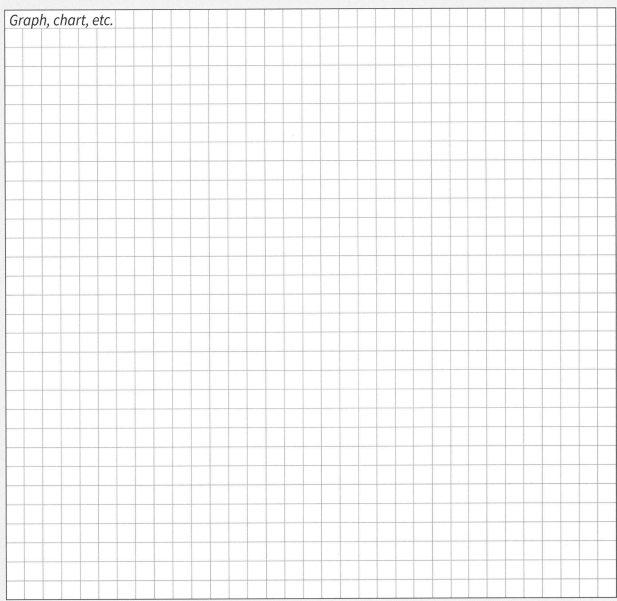

c. Analysing data

Calculations, trends, etc.

4. Investigation evaluation

5. Investigation conclusion

6. References

7. Key skills development

Key skills	How I developed these skills during this task

Scientific Investigation

Title:

Nature of Science ☐
Biological World ☐
Chemical World ☐
Physical World ☐
Earth and Space ☐

Chapter number:

Page number:

Date:

Lab partner(s):

1. Introduction to investigation and background information

Hypothesis

2. Investigation design

Variables

a. Independent variable

b. Dependent variable

c. Controlled (fixed) variables

d. Control (if necessary)

Equipment

Method

Labelled diagram

Safety

3. Investigation results

a. Obtaining and recording data

Table

b. Presenting data

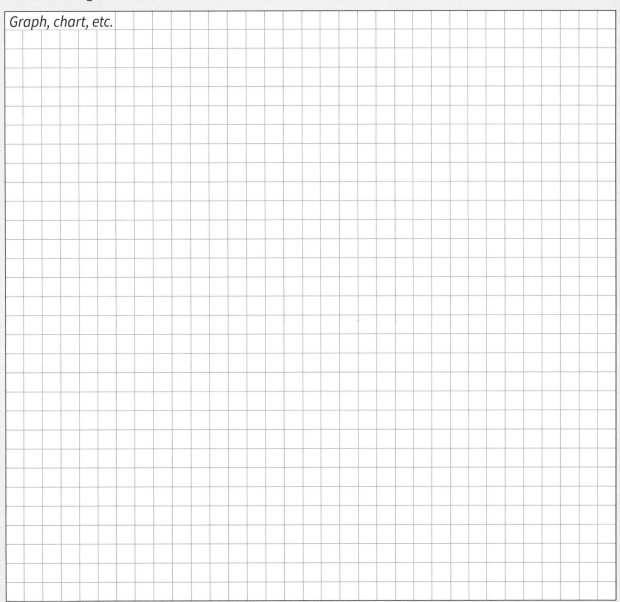

Graph, chart, etc.

c. Analysing data

Calculations, trends, etc.

4. Investigation evaluation

5. Investigation conclusion

6. References

7. Key skills development

Key skills	How I developed these skills during this task

Science in Society

Science in Society

Title: ....

Biological World	☐
Chemical World	☐
Physical World	☐
Earth and Space	☐

Chapter number: ....

Page number: ....

Date: ....

Lab partner(s): ....

....

1. Issue to be considered

2. Explanation of key scientific ideas related to the issue. What are the big ideas related to this issue?

3. What research needs to be done around this issue? State your sources and summarise the key points you found out from them.

   Source 1:

Source 2:

Source 3:

Source 4:

4. Processing information

Scribble box: pros	*Scribble box: cons*

5. Evaluation of data and information

Summarise what you have learned about this issue.

a. Do you need to take a position in relation to this issue? State what your position is and why.

b. Present the findings that support your position.

6. Conclusion

a. Looking forward: potential concerns

b. Looking forward: potential benefits

c. Recommendations

7. References

8. Key skills development

Key skills	How I developed these skills during this task

Science in Society

Title:...

Biological World ☐

Chemical World ☐

Physical World ☐

Earth and Space ☐

Chapter number: ....

Page number: ....

Date:...

Lab partner(s):..

....

1. Issue to be considered

---

2. Explanation of key scientific ideas related to the issue. What are the big ideas related to this issue?

---

3. What research needs to be done around this issue? State your sources and summarise the key points you found out from them.

Source 1:

Source 2:

Source 3:

Source 4:

4. Processing information

Scribble box: pros	*Scribble box: cons*

5. Evaluation of data and information

Summarise what you have learned about this issue.

a. Do you need to take a position in relation to this issue? State what your position is and why.

b. Present the findings that support your position.

6. Conclusion

a. Looking forward: potential concerns

b. Looking forward: potential benefits

c. Recommendations

7. References

8. Key skills development

Key skills	How I developed these skills during this task

Science in Society

Title:..

Biological World ☐

Chemical World ☐

Physical World ☐

Earth and Space ☐

Chapter number: ....

Page number: ....

Date:..

Lab partner(s):..

....

1. Issue to be considered

2. Explanation of key scientific ideas related to the issue. What are the big ideas related to this issue?

3. What research needs to be done around this issue? State your sources and summarise the key points you found out from them.

Source 1:

Source 2:

Source 3:

Source 4:

4. Processing information

Scribble box: pros	*Scribble box: cons*

5. Evaluation of data and information

Summarise what you have learned about this issue.

a. Do you need to take a position in relation to this issue? State what your position is and why.

b. Present the findings that support your position.

6. Conclusion

a. Looking forward: potential concerns

b. Looking forward: potential benefits

c. Recommendations

7. References

8. Key skills development

Key skills	**How I developed these skills during this task**

Science in Society

Title:..

Biological World	☐	Chapter number: ....
Chemical World	☐	Page number: ....
Physical World	☐	Date: ....
Earth and Space	☐	Lab partner(s): ....

....

1. Issue to be considered

____

____

____

____

____

2. Explanation of key scientific ideas related to the issue. What are the big ideas related to this issue?

____

____

____

____

____

____

3. What research needs to be done around this issue? State your sources and summarise the key points you found out from them.

Source 1:

____

____

____

____

Source 2:

Source 3:

Source 4:

4. Processing information

Scribble box: pros	*Scribble box: cons*

5. Evaluation of data and information

Summarise what you have learned about this issue.

a. Do you need to take a position in relation to this issue? State what your position is and why.

b. Present the findings that support your position.

6. Conclusion

a. Looking forward: potential concerns

b. Looking forward: potential benefits

c. Recommendations

7. References

8. Key skills development

Key skills	How I developed these skills during this task

Science in Society

Title: ....

Biological World ☐

Chemical World ☐

Physical World ☐

Earth and Space ☐

Chapter number: ....

Page number: ....

Date: ....

Lab partner(s): ....

....

1. Issue to be considered

2. Explanation of key scientific ideas related to the issue. What are the big ideas related to this issue?

3. What research needs to be done around this issue? State your sources and summarise the key points you found out from them.

Source 1:

Source 2:

Source 3:

Source 4:

4. Processing information

Scribble box: pros	*Scribble box: cons*

5. Evaluation of data and information

Summarise what you have learned about this issue.

a. Do you need to take a position in relation to this issue? State what your position is and why.

b. Present the findings that support your position.

6. Conclusion

a. Looking forward: potential concerns

b. Looking forward: potential benefits

c. Recommendations

7. References

8. Key skills development

Key skills	How I developed these skills during this task

Science in Society

Title: ....

Biological World	☐
Chemical World	☐
Physical World	☐
Earth and Space	☐

Chapter number: ....

Page number: ....

Date: ....

Lab partner(s): ....

....

1. Issue to be considered

2. Explanation of key scientific ideas related to the issue. What are the big ideas related to this issue?

3. What research needs to be done around this issue? State your sources and summarise the key points you found out from them.

Source 1:

Source 2:

Source 3:

Source 4:

4. Processing information

Scribble box: pros	*Scribble box: cons*

5. Evaluation of data and information

Summarise what you have learned about this issue.

a. Do you need to take a position in relation to this issue? State what your position is and why.

b. Present the findings that support your position.

6. Conclusion

a. Looking forward: potential concerns

b. Looking forward: potential benefits

c. Recommendations

7. References

8. Key skills development

Key skills	How I developed these skills during this task

Science in Society

Title:..

Biological World ☐

Chemical World ☐

Physical World ☐

Earth and Space ☐

Chapter number: ....

Page number: ....

Date:..

Lab partner(s):..

....

1. Issue to be considered

____

____

____

____

____

2. Explanation of key scientific ideas related to the issue. What are the big ideas related to this issue?

____

____

____

____

____

____

3. What research needs to be done around this issue? State your sources and summarise the key points you found out from them.

Source 1:

____

____

____

____

Source 2:

Source 3:

Source 4:

4. Processing information

Scribble box: pros	*Scribble box: cons*

5. Evaluation of data and information

Summarise what you have learned about this issue.

a. Do you need to take a position in relation to this issue? State what your position is and why.

b. Present the findings that support your position.

6. Conclusion

a. Looking forward: potential concerns

b. Looking forward: potential benefits

c. Recommendations

7. References

8. Key skills development

Key skills	**How I developed these skills during this task**

Science in Society

Title: ....

Biological World ☐
Chemical World ☐
Physical World ☐
Earth and Space ☐

Chapter number: ....

Page number: ....

Date: ....

Lab partner(s): ....

....

1. Issue to be considered

2. Explanation of key scientific ideas related to the issue. What are the big ideas related to this issue?

3. What research needs to be done around this issue? State your sources and summarise the key points you found out from them.

Source 1:

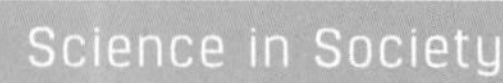

Source 2:

Source 3:

Source 4:

4. Processing information

Scribble box: pros	*Scribble box: cons*

5. Evaluation of data and information

Summarise what you have learned about this issue.

a. Do you need to take a position in relation to this issue? State what your position is and why.

b. Present the findings that support your position.

6. Conclusion

a. Looking forward: potential concerns

b. Looking forward: potential benefits

c. Recommendations

7. References

8. Key skills development

Key skills	How I developed these skills during this task

Science in Society

Title: ....

Biological World ☐

Chemical World ☐

Physical World ☐

Earth and Space ☐

Chapter number: ....

Page number: ....

Date: ....

Lab partner(s): ....

....

1. Issue to be considered

2. Explanation of key scientific ideas related to the issue. What are the big ideas related to this issue?

3. What research needs to be done around this issue? State your sources and summarise the key points you found out from them.

Source 1:

Source 2:

Source 3:

Source 4:

4. Processing information

Scribble box: pros	*Scribble box: cons*

5. Evaluation of data and information

Summarise what you have learned about this issue.

a. Do you need to take a position in relation to this issue? State what your position is and why.

b. Present the findings that support your position.

6. Conclusion

a. Looking forward: potential concerns

b. Looking forward: potential benefits

c. Recommendations

7. References

8. Key skills development

Key skills	**How I developed these skills during this task**

Science in Society

Title: ....

Biological World	☐	Chapter number: ....
Chemical World	☐	Page number: ....
Physical World	☐	Date: ....
Earth and Space	☐	Lab partner(s): ....
		....

1. Issue to be considered

2. Explanation of key scientific ideas related to the issue. What are the big ideas related to this issue?

3. What research needs to be done around this issue? State your sources and summarise the key points you found out from them.

Source 1:

Source 2:

Source 3:

Source 4:

4. Processing information

Scribble box: pros	*Scribble box: cons*

5. Evaluation of data and information

Summarise what you have learned about this issue.

a. Do you need to take a position in relation to this issue? State what your position is and why.

b. Present the findings that support your position.

6. Conclusion

a. Looking forward: potential concerns

b. Looking forward: potential benefits

c. Recommendations

7. References

8. Key skills development

Key skills	How I developed these skills during this task

Check Your Learning

Check Your Learning

When you have completed a topic, it is important to check what you have learned and how well you have understood it. It is also important to plan when you will review each topic in future.

The traffic light system

Use the traffic light system to help you check your learning and understanding of each topic. Each time you review a topic, choose the colour that most closely matches how you feel about what you have learned. Review each topic and tick your level until you get to green, and record the date of the review.

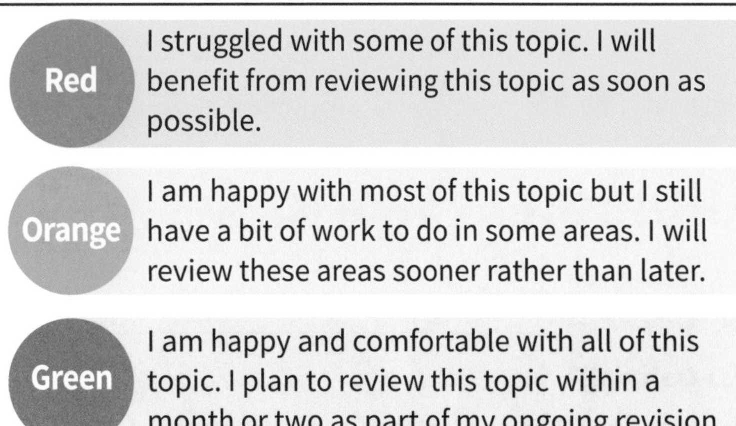
Red
I struggled with some of this topic. I will benefit from reviewing this topic as soon as possible.
Orange
I am happy with most of this topic but I still have a bit of work to do in some areas. I will review these areas sooner rather than later.
Green
I am happy and comfortable with all of this topic. I plan to review this topic within a month or two as part of my ongoing revision.

Introduction: Nature of Science

0.1 What is Science?

- Consider science as a process that allows people to investigate natural occurrences (phenomena) that can be tested.
- Describe how science gives us a body of knowledge that is always changing.

Review 1: ● ● ● (/ /); Review 2: ● ● ● (/ /); Review 3: ● ● ● (/ /)

0.2 Investigation Design

- Distinguish between the different types of variables and a control.
- Explain how to produce a fair and reliable method to carry out an investigation.
- Discuss the importance of laboratory safety and ethics.

Review 1: ● ● ● (/ /); Review 2: ● ● ● (/ /); Review 3: ● ● ● (/ /)

0.3 Recording, Presenting and Analysing Data

- Explain the difference between quantitative and qualitative data.
- Present data in tables and graphs.
- Interpret data and draw conclusions.

Review 1: ● ● ● (/ /); Review 2: ● ● ● (/ /); Review 3: ● ● ● (/ /)

0.4 Communication, Teamwork and Responsible Science

- Outline the different ways to communicate scientific knowledge.
- Review the role of models when communicating scientific information.
- Evaluate scientific information.
- Reflect on the importance of teamwork and responsibility in science.

Review 1: ● ● ● (/ /); Review 2: ● ● ● (/ /); Review 3: ● ● ● (/ /)

Biological World

Chapter 1 The Organisation of Life

1.1 Defining Life

- Identify seven characteristics common to living organisms.

Review 1: ● ● ● (/ /); Review 2: ● ● ● (/ /); Review 3: ● ● ● (/ /)

1.2 The Cell and Light Microscope

- Identify cells as the 'building blocks' of all organisms and tell the difference between unicellular and multicellular organisms.
- Name the parts of a light microscope and explain what they do.
- Prepare slides using onion cells and view them under a light microscope.

Review 1: ● ● ● (/ /); Review 2: ● ● ● (/ /); Review 3: ● ● ● (/ /)

1.3 The Structure of the Cell

- Compare plant and animal cells.
- Outline the role of cell organelles, including the cell membrane, cytoplasm and nucleus.

Review 1: ● ● ● (/ /); Review 2: ● ● ● (/ /); Review 3: ● ● ● (/ /)

1.4 Organisation of Life

- Outline the stages of organisation in living organisms.

Review 1: ● ● ● (/ /); Review 2: ● ● ● (/ /); Review 3: ● ● ● (/ /)

Chapter 2 The Chemicals of Life

2.1 Biomolecules and Food Tests

- Describe how food supplies organisms with the energy they need.
- Conduct investigations to find out the biomolecules present in different foods.

Review 1: ● ● ● (/ /); Review 2: ● ● ● (/ /); Review 3: ● ● ● (/ /)

2.2 The Importance of a Balanced Diet

- Consider why one diet does not suit everyone.
- Interpret food labels.
- Plan a balanced diet to promote good health.

Review 1: ● ● ● (/ /); Review 2: ● ● ● (/ /); Review 3: ● ● ● (/ /)

2.3 Malnutrition

- Justify the importance of a balanced diet, regular exercise and rest.
- Discuss how malnutrition and poor lifestyle choices may lead to health problems.
- Identify the causes and symptoms of various dietary and lifestyle diseases.

Review 1: ● ● ● (/ /); Review 2: ● ● ● (/ /); Review 3: ● ● ● (/ /)

Chapter 3 The Energy of Life

3.1 Metabolism, Enzymes and Homeostasis

- Explain the role of energy and its changes in living organisms.
- Describe the role of enzymes in controlling chemical reactions in cells.
- Explain how organisms achieve homeostasis.

Review 1: ● ● ● (/ /); Review 2: ● ● ● (/ /); Review 3: ● ● ● (/ /)

3.2 Photosynthesis

- Outline the role of photosynthesis in controlling the flow of energy and cycling of matter through the Earth.
- Formulate a word equation for photosynthesis.
- Investigate the environmental factors that affect the rate of photosynthesis.

Review 1: ● ● ● (/ /); Review 2: ● ● ● (/ /); Review 3: ● ● ● (/ /)

3.3 Respiration

- Recognise that all organisms respire and explain the role of energy for organisms.
- Formulate a word equation for respiration.
- Evaluate the role of respiration and photosynthesis in the flow of energy and cycling of matter through the Earth.

Review 1: ● ● ● (/ /); Review 2: ● ● ● (/ /); Review 3: ● ● ● (/ /)

Chapter 4 The Continuity of Life: Genetics and Evolution

4.1 Genetics

- Distinguish the difference between inherited and acquired characteristics.
- Recognise that a gene is the basic unit of inheritance.
- Appreciate the role of Gregor Mendel in developing our understanding of inheritance and consider a simple genetic cross.

Review 1: ● ● ● (/ /); Review 2: ● ● ● (/ /); Review 3: ● ● ● (/ /)

4.2 Variation and Evolution

- Analyse the role of environmental and genetic factors in variation.
- Use Darwin's theory of evolution by natural selection to explain the diversity of organisms.

Review 1: ● ● ● (/ /); Review 2: ● ● ● (/ /); Review 3: ● ● ● (/ /)

4.3 Mutation

- Examine how mutation introduces variation into a population.
- Explain the causes and treatments for certain cancers.
- Consider the role of mutation and inheritance in common genetic disorders.

Review 1: ● ● ● (/ /); Review 2: ● ● ● (/ /); Review 3: ● ● ● (/ /)

4.4 Genetic Engineering and Cloning

- Research the arguments for and against genetic engineering.

Review 1: ● ● ● (/ /); Review 2: ● ● ● (/ /); Review 3: ● ● ● (/ /)

Chapter 5 The Diversity of Life

5.1 The Five Kingdoms of Life

- List the five kingdoms of life.
- Describe how organisms are classified.

Review 1: ● ● ● (/ /); Review 2: ● ● ● (/ /); Review 3: ● ● ● (/ /)

5.2 Bacteria and Viruses

- Describe the defining features of bacteria and viruses.
- Consider the important role that bacteria play as producers and decomposers.
- Discuss the role of bacteria and viruses as disease-causing organisms.

Review 1: ● ● ● (/ /); Review 2: ● ● ● (/ /); Review 3: ● ● ● (/ /)

Chapter 6 The Interactions of Life: Ecology

6.1 The Structure of an Ecosystem

- Recognise an ecosystem as the relationship between organisms and their environment.
- Illustrate the levels of organisation in an ecosystem.

Review 1: ● ● ● (/ /); Review 2: ● ● ● (/ /); Review 3: ● ● ● (/ /)

6.2 Interactions of Organisms in an Ecosystem

- Identify how organisms interact with the non-living environment.
- Consider how organisms also interact with each other in different ways.

Review 1: ● ● ● (/ /); Review 2: ● ● ● (/ /); Review 3: ● ● ● (/ /)

6.3 Adaptations of Organisms in an Ecosystem

- Compare the adaptations of different organisms to suit their habitats.

Review 1: ● ● ● (/ /); Review 2: ● ● ● (/ /); Review 3: ● ● ● (/ /)

6.4 Feeding Relationships in an Ecosystem

- Model the flow of energy through an ecosystem using a food chain and a food web.
- Review the importance of decomposers to the cycling of key nutrients through the living and non-living parts of the Earth.

Review 1: ● ● ● (/ /); Review 2: ● ● ● (/ /); Review 3: ● ● ● (/ /)

6.5 Conducting a Habitat Study

- Choose the appropriate equipment and techniques to safely survey a habitat.
- Conduct a local habitat study.

Review 1: ● ● ● (/ /); Review 2: ● ● ● (/ /); Review 3: ● ● ● (/ /)

Chapter 7 Structures and Processes of Life: Plants

7.1 The Structure of Flowering Plants

- Classify the four plant organs: root, stem, leaf and flower.
- Explain how plant organs are adapted to perform special roles.

Review 1: ● ● ● (/ /); Review 2: ● ● ● (/ /); Review 3: ● ● ● (/ /)

7.2 The Processes of Flowering Plants

- Outline the role of xylem and phloem tissue in plants.
- Recognise the role played by stomata in the exchange of gases with the atmosphere.
- Investigate the response of plants to changes in their environment.

Review 1: ● ● ● (/ /); Review 2: ● ● ● (/ /); Review 3: ● ● ● (/ /)

7.3 Asexual Reproduction in Flowering Plants

- Explore various ways that plants may reproduce asexually.
- Describe artificial methods of asexual reproduction in plants practised in agriculture and horticulture.

Review 1: ● ● ● (/ /); Review 2: ● ● ● (/ /); Review 3: ● ● ● (/ /)

7.4 Sexual Reproduction in Flowering Plants

- Examine the role of the flower in the sexual reproduction of plants.
- Outline the stages involved in the sexual reproduction of plants.

Review 1: ● ● ● (/ /); Review 2: ● ● ● (/ /); Review 3: ● ● ● (/ /)

Chapter 8 Structures and Processes of Life: Humans

8.1 The Organisation of Humans

- Recognise that humans are multicellular organisms that demonstrate significant levels of organisation.
- Discuss the role of each system within the human body.

Review 1: ● ● ● (/ /); Review 2: ● ● ● (/ /); Review 3: ● ● ● (/ /)

8.2 The Digestive System

- Identify that humans are consumers and must eat and digest food.
- Identify and explain the roles of the organs of the digestive system.
- Explore the health of the human digestive system.

Review 1: ● ● ● (/ /); Review 2: ● ● ● (/ /); Review 3: ● ● ● (/ /)

8.3 The Circulatory System

- Identify and explain the roles of the organs of the circulatory system.
- Explore the health of the human circulatory system.

Review 1: ● ● ● (/ /); Review 2: ● ● ● (/ /); Review 3: ● ● ● (/ /)

8.4 The Respiratory System

- Identify and explain the roles of the organs of the respiratory system.
- Explore the health of the human respiratory system.

Review 1: ● ● ● (/ /); Review 2: ● ● ● (/ /); Review 3: ● ● ● (/ /)

8.5 The Reproductive System

- Identify and explain the roles of the organs of the female and male reproductive systems.
- Explore the health of the female and male reproductive systems.
- Research issues surrounding human reproduction.

Review 1: ● ● ● (/ /); Review 2: ● ● ● (/ /); Review 3: ● ● ● (/ /)

Chemical World

Chapter 9 What Matter is Made Of

9.1 The Particle Theory and States of Matter

- Recognise that matter is made up of particles.
- Describe the properties of solids, liquids and gases.
- Use the particle theory to explain the properties of solids, liquids and gases.

Review 1: ● ● ● (/ /); Review 2: ● ● ● (/ /); Review 3: ● ● ● (/ /)

9.2 Diffusion

- Model the diffusion of a gas using the particle theory.

Review 1: ● ● ● (/ /); Review 2: ● ● ● (/ /); Review 3: ● ● ● (/ /)

9.3 Changes of State

- Use the particle theory to explain changes of state involving solids, liquids and gases.
- Explain the following terms: melting, boiling, evaporation, condensation, freezing and sublimation.
- Interpret data to find out the state of a substance at various temperatures.

Review 1: ● ● ● (/ /); Review 2: ● ● ● (/ /); Review 3: ● ● ● (/ /)

9.4 Properties of Materials

- Investigate the properties of various materials.
- Conduct research on the recycling habits of your classmates.

Review 1: ● ● ● (/ /); Review 2: ● ● ● (/ /); Review 3: ● ● ● (/ /)

9.5 Physical Change Versus Chemical Change

- Distinguish between physical and chemical changes.
- Investigate whether mass is changed or unchanged when chemical and physical changes take place.
- Verify the law of conservation of mass.

Review 1: ● ● ● (/ /); Review 2: ● ● ● (/ /); Review 3: ● ● ● (/ /)

Chapter 10 The Building Blocks of the Chemical World

10.1 Atoms and Elements

- Outline how our understanding of matter has evolved over time.
- Explain what an element is.
- Identify the chemical symbols for a number of elements.

Review 1: ● ● ● (/ /); Review 2: ● ● ● (/ /); Review 3: ● ● ● (/ /)

10.2 Subatomic Particles

- Calculate the number of protons, neutrons and electrons in an atom using the atomic number and mass number.
- Classify protons, neutrons and electrons in terms of mass, charge and location in the atom.

Review 1: ● ● ● (/ /); Review 2: ● ● ● (/ /); Review 3: ● ● ● (/ /)

10.3 Atomic Structure

- Develop a model to help explain the basic structure of an atom.
- Reflect on the contribution of Niels Bohr to atomic theory.

Review 1: ● ● ● (/ /); Review 2: ● ● ● (/ /); Review 3: ● ● ● (/ /)

10.4 The Periodic Table of the Elements

- Outline the contribution of John Newlands and Dmitri Mendeleev in developing the periodic table.
- Describe and explain the structure of the periodic table.

Review 1: ● ● ● (/ /); Review 2: ● ● ● (/ /); Review 3: ● ● ● (/ /)

10.5 Metals and Non-Metals

- Classify an element as a metal or a non-metal using the periodic table.
- Investigate the properties of metals and non-metals.
- Describe what an alloy is and give examples of common alloys.

Review 1: ● ● ● (/ /); Review 2: ● ● ● (/ /); Review 3: ● ● ● (/ /)

Chapter 11 Compounds, Mixtures and Solutions

11.1 Compounds and Mixtures

- Distinguish between pure and impure substances.
- Investigate the difference between elements, compounds and mixtures using models.

Review 1: ● ● ● (/ /); Review 2: ● ● ● (/ /); Review 3: ● ● ● (/ /)

11.2 Solutions

- Explain the terms solute, solvent and solution and how they relate to each other.
- Measure the solubility of different solids at different temperatures.

Review 1: ● ● ● (/ /); Review 2: ● ● ● (/ /); Review 3: ● ● ● (/ /)

11.3 Crystallisation

- Compare concentrated and saturated solutions.
- Investigate and demonstrate crystallisation.

Review 1: ● ● ● (/ /); Review 2: ● ● ● (/ /); Review 3: ● ● ● (/ /)

11.4 Separating Mixtures

- Separate various mixtures using appropriate techniques.
- Examine the various by-products of separation.
- Investigate the advantages and disadvantages of fracking as a means of extracting natural gas.

Review 1: ● ● ● (/ /); Review 2: ● ● ● (/ /); Review 3: ● ● ● (/ /)

Chapter 12 Chemical Reactions: Fast and Slow

12.1 Chemical Reactions

- Describe a chemical reaction.
- Observe and record changes that occur during chemical reactions.

Review 1: ● ● ● (/ /); Review 2: ● ● ● (/ /); Review 3: ● ● ● (/ /)

12.2 Endothermic and Exothermic Reactions

- Distinguish between endothermic and exothermic chemical reactions.
- Produce an energy profile diagram for endothermic and exothermic reactions.

Review 1: ● ● ● (/ /); Review 2: ● ● ● (/ /); Review 3: ● ● ● (/ /)

12.3 How Do Chemical Reactions Happen?

- Explain activation energy.
- Consider how the rate of a chemical reaction can be monitored over time.
- Interpret a rate of reaction graph.

Review 1: ● ● ● (/ /); Review 2: ● ● ● (/ /); Review 3: ● ● ● (/ /)

12.4 Factors Affecting the Rate of a Reaction

- Identify a number of factors that affect the rate of chemical reactions.
- Use the collision theory to explain how certain factors influence the rate of a chemical reaction.
- Produce and interpret rate of reaction graphs.

Review 1: ● ● ● (/ /); Review 2: ● ● ● (/ /); Review 3: ● ● ● (/ /)

12.5 Production of Gases

- Produce and test for the presence of oxygen and carbon dioxide gases.
- Design an investigation to verify that surface area and particle size affect the rate of a reaction.
- Investigate how the presence of a catalyst affects the rate of reaction.

Review 1: ● ● ● (/ /); Review 2: ● ● ● (/ /); Review 3: ● ● ● (/ /)

Chapter 13 Acids and Bases

13.1 Acids and Bases

- List examples of everyday acids and bases.
- Discuss how concentrated acids and bases should be handled safely.
- Distinguish between dilute and concentrated solutions of an acid.

Review 1: ● ● ● (/ /); Review 2: ● ● ● (/ /); Review 3: ● ● ● (/ /)

13.2 pH and Indicators

- Investigate the concentrations of dilute and concentrated acids and alkalis using the pH scale.
- Produce an acid–base indicator from plant material.

Review 1: ● ● ● (/ /); Review 2: ● ● ● (/ /); Review 3: ● ● ● (/ /)

13.3 Neutralisation

- Plan and carry out a titration between hydrochloric acid and sodium hydroxide.
- Measure pH changes in neutralisation reactions.
- List everyday examples of neutralisation reactions.

Review 1: ● ● ● (/ /); Review 2: ● ● ● (/ /); Review 3: ● ● ● (/ /)

Chapter 14 Chemical Reactions: Bonding

14.1 Types of Chemical Reactions

- Outline and explain different types of chemical reactions.
- Apply the law of conservation of mass to chemical reactions.
- Investigate combustion reactions.

Review 1: ● ● ● (/ /); Review 2: ● ● ● (/ /); Review 3: ● ● ● (/ /)

14.2 Reactions of Metals

- Describe the reactions of the alkali and alkaline earth metals.
- Identify the conditions needed for corrosion of metals.
- Organise metals according to how reactive they are with water and dilute acid.

Review 1: ● ● ● (/ /); Review 2: ● ● ● (/ /); Review 3: ● ● ● (/ /)

14.3 Atoms in Reactions

- Explain how atoms in elements can be rearranged to form new substances.
- Recognise the difference between ionic and covalent bonding.
- Investigate the properties of ionic and covalent substances.

Review 1: ● ● ● (/ /); Review 2: ● ● ● (/ /); Review 3: ● ● ● (/ /)

14.4 Chemical Formulae

- Predict the ratio of elements in a compound using the periodic table.
- Produce chemical formulae for compounds of two elements.

Review 1: ● ● ● (/ /); Review 2: ● ● ● (/ /); Review 3: ● ● ● (/ /)

Physical World

Chapter 15 Measuring the Physical World

15.1 SI Units

- Explain what is meant by physical quantity.
- Identify SI units of measurement for different physical quantities.
- Compare basic SI units with derived SI units.

Review 1: ● ● ● (/ /); Review 2: ● ● ● (/ /); Review 3: ● ● ● (/ /)

15.2 Measuring Length and Area

- Describe how to use various instruments for measuring length.
- Measure and calculate the area of a regular and irregular shape.

Review 1: ● ● ● (/ /); Review 2: ● ● ● (/ /); Review 3: ● ● ● (/ /)

15.3 Measuring Mass and Volume

- Define mass and volume.
- Describe ways to measure the mass of different objects.
- Outline the correct use of a graduated cylinder and investigate how to measure the volume of regular- and irregular-shaped objects.

Review 1: ● ● ● (/ /); Review 2: ● ● ● (/ /); Review 3: ● ● ● (/ /)

15.4 Accuracy in Measurements

- Distinguish between random and systematic errors.
- Reflect on how random and systematic errors can be reduced.

Review 1: ● ● ● (/ /); Review 2: ● ● ● (/ /); Review 3: ● ● ● (/ /)

Chapter 16 Energy

16.1 What is Energy?

- Explain what energy is.
- Illustrate ways that energy can be stored.
- State the law of conservation of energy.

Review 1: ● ● ● (/ /); Review 2: ● ● ● (/ /); Review 3: ● ● ● (/ /)

16.2 Energy Transfers

- Distinguish between useful and waste energy conversions.
- Interpret models for representing energy transfers.
- Calculate the efficiency of different devices.

Review 1: ● ● ● (/ /); Review 2: ● ● ● (/ /); Review 3: ● ● ● (/ /)

16.3 Energy Transfer in the Home

- Explain what is meant by power.
- Calculate the power of different electrical appliances.
- Outline steps that can be taken to make homes more energy efficient.

Review 1: ● ● ● (/ /); Review 2: ● ● ● (/ /); Review 3: ● ● ● (/ /)

Chapter 17 Motion

17.1 Types of Motion

- Distinguish between scalar and vector quantities.
- Measure and calculate length, time, speed, displacement and velocity.
- Interpret relationships between distance and time for moving objects.

Review 1: ● ● ● (/ /); Review 2: ● ● ● (/ /); Review 3: ● ● ● (/ /)

17.2 Changing Speeds

- Consider what it means for an object to accelerate.
- Measure and calculate accelerations.
- Predict the motion of objects experiencing accelerations.

Review 1: ● ● ● (/ /); Review 2: ● ● ● (/ /); Review 3: ● ● ● (/ /)

17.3 Forces: Pushes and Pulls

- Classify forces as contact and non-contact.
- Describe various interaction pairs.
- Demonstrate a way to measure forces.

Review 1: ● ● ● (/ /); Review 2: ● ● ● (/ /); Review 3: ● ● ● (/ /)

17.4 Forces: Moving Faster and Slower

- Compare balanced and unbalanced forces.
- Discuss useful and nuisance friction effects.
- Explore streamlining in nature and technology.

Review 1: ● ● ● (/ /); Review 2: ● ● ● (/ /); Review 3: ● ● ● (/ /)

17.5 Forces: Changing Shapes

- Describe how solids support weight.
- Model how forces deform objects.

Review 1: ● ● ● (/ /); Review 2: ● ● ● (/ /); Review 3: ● ● ● (/ /)

17.6 Forces: Pressure

- Measure and calculate pressures.
- Outline how pressure varies in liquids and gases.
- Explain what is meant by atmospheric pressure.

Review 1: ● ● ● (/ /); Review 2: ● ● ● (/ /); Review 3: ● ● ● (/ /)

17.7 Forces: Floating and Sinking

- Measure and calculate density.
- Evaluate the relationship between density and floating bodies.
- Illustrate how bodies experience upthrust.

Review 1: ● ● ● (/ /); Review 2: ● ● ● (/ /); Review 3: ● ● ● (/ /)

Chapter 18 Magnetism and Electricity

18.1 Magnetism

- Investigate the properties of magnets.
- Evaluate the nature and role of magnetic fields.
- Illustrate magnetic field lines using a plotting compass.

Review 1: ● ● ● (/ /); Review 2: ● ● ● (/ /); Review 3: ● ● ● (/ /)

18.2 What is Electricity?

- Demonstrate that electricity is a form of energy.
- Investigate the differences between conductors and insulators.
- Distinguish between static and current electricity.

Review 1: ● ● ● (/ /); Review 2: ● ● ● (/ /); Review 3: ● ● ● (/ /)

18.3 Static Charges

- Discuss how objects can be charged by friction.
- Investigate the interaction between like and unlike charged particles.

Review 1: ● ● ● (/ /); Review 2: ● ● ● (/ /); Review 3: ● ● ● (/ /)

18.4 Effects of Static Electricity

- Examine how lightning occurs and how lightning conductors work.
- Outline some uses of static electricity.

Review 1: ● ● ● (/ /); Review 2: ● ● ● (/ /); Review 3: ● ● ● (/ /)

18.5 Electric Circuits

- Explain what is meant by electric current.
- Plan, design and build simple electric circuits.
- Model the basic operation of an electric circuit.

Review 1: ● ● ● (/ /); Review 2: ● ● ● (/ /); Review 3: ● ● ● (/ /)

18.6 Potential Difference and Voltage

- Model potential difference in electric circuits.
- Identify different sources of potential difference.

Review 1: ● ● ● (/ /); Review 2: ● ● ● (/ /); Review 3: ● ● ● (/ /)

18.7 Series and Parallel Circuits

- Distinguish between the wiring of components in series and parallel circuits.
- Compare voltages and currents in series and parallel circuits.

Review 1: ● ● ● (/ /); Review 2: ● ● ● (/ /); Review 3: ● ● ● (/ /)

18.8 Resistance

- Appreciate what resistance means.
- Calculate voltage, current and resistance in electric circuits.
- Investigate the factors that affect the resistance of a component.

Review 1: ● ● ● (/ /); Review 2: ● ● ● (/ /); Review 3: ● ● ● (/ /)

18.9 Electricity in the Home

- Illustrate how appliances are connected to the mains supply.
- Distinguish between alternating current and direct current.
- Investigate the role of a fuse wire.

Review 1: ● ● ● (/ /); Review 2: ● ● ● (/ /); Review 3: ● ● ● (/ /)

Chapter 19 Seeing, Hearing, Feeling

19.1 Bouncing Light

- Demonstrate that light is a form of energy.
- Conduct an investigation on the reflection of light off mirrors.

Review 1: ● ● ● (/ /); Review 2: ● ● ● (/ /); Review 3: ● ● ● (/ /)

19.2 Bending Light

- Evaluate a model for refraction of light.
- Investigate the refraction of light through different solids.
- Describe how our eyes allow us to see.

Review 1: ● ● ● (/ /); Review 2: ● ● ● (/ /); Review 3: ● ● ● (/ /)

19.3 Splitting Light

- Explain the process of dispersion.
- Distinguish between primary and secondary colours.
- Review how we see coloured objects.

Review 1: ● ● ● (/ /); Review 2: ● ● ● (/ /); Review 3: ● ● ● (/ /)

19.4 Sound

- Compare the speed of sound with the speed of light.
- Examine the factors that affect the pitch and loudness of a sound.
- Explore the importance of sound safety.

Review 1: ● ● ● (/ /); Review 2: ● ● ● (/ /); Review 3: ● ● ● (/ /)

19.5 Heat Transfer

- Investigate the ways in which heat moves through solids, liquids and gases.
- Distinguish between conductors and insulators of heat.
- Compare the colour of an object with its ability to absorb and emit radiated heat.

Review 1: ● ● ● (/ /); Review 2: ● ● ● (/ /); Review 3: ● ● ● (/ /)

19.6 Effects of Heat

- Investigate the expansion and contraction of substances with heat.
- Review examples of the expansion and contraction of solids in the real world.

Review 1: ● ● ● (/ /); Review 2: ● ● ● (/ /); Review 3: ● ● ● (/ /)

Chapter 20 The Modern Physical World

20.1 The Information Age

- Discuss the differences between analogue and digital signals.
- Describe how processors can store and transfer information.
- Explore the impact of modern technologies on our daily lives.

Review 1: ● ● ● (/ /); Review 2: ● ● ● (/ /); Review 3: ● ● ● (/ /)

20.2 Physics and Health

- Produce an electric circuit that can be used to monitor body temperature.
- Describe how ultrasound and MRI scanning work.

Review 1: ● ● ● (/ /); Review 2: ● ● ● (/ /); Review 3: ● ● ● (/ /)

20.3 Fast Physics

- Model the collision of particles in a particle accelerator.
- Research the work being done at CERN.

Review 1: ● ● ● (/ /); Review 2: ● ● ● (/ /); Review 3: ● ● ● (/ /)

Earth and Space

Chapter 21 Space

21.1 Origins of the Universe

- Outline how our understanding of the universe has changed over time.
- Explore a scientific model to illustrate the origin of the universe.
- Describe the different types of celestial bodies that exist.

Review 1: ● ● ● (/ /); Review 2: ● ● ● (/ /); Review 3: ● ● ● (/ /)

21.2 Celestial Bodies

- Distinguish between celestial bodies and give examples.
- Interpret data to compare various celestial bodies.

Review 1: ● ● ● (/ /); Review 2: ● ● ● (/ /); Review 3: ● ● ● (/ /)

21.3 The Planets in Our Solar System

- List the planets in the solar system.
- Compare the Earth with other planets in terms of mass, gravity, size and composition.
- Appreciate that gravity is a force that binds the universe together.

Review 1: ● ● ● (/ /); Review 2: ● ● ● (/ /); Review 3: ● ● ● (/ /)

Chapter 22 Earth

22.1 The Structure of the Earth

- Name the three layers that make up the Earth.
- Describe plate tectonics and seismology.
- Identify the three types of rock that the Earth's crust is composed of: igneous, sedimentary and metamorphic.

Review 1: ● ● ● (/ /); Review 2: ● ● ● (/ /); Review 3: ● ● ● (/ /)

22.2 The Cycling of Matter

- Consider the cycling of matter through the living and non-living parts of the Earth.
- Review models for the cycling of carbon and nitrogen.

Review 1: ● ● ● (/ /); Review 2: ● ● ● (/ /); Review 3: ● ● ● (/ /)

22.3 Water

- Examine the properties and roles of water.
- Outline how water cycles through the living and non-living parts of the Earth.
- Investigate the electrolysis of water.

Review 1: ● ● ● (/ /); Review 2: ● ● ● (/ /); Review 3: ● ● ● (/ /)

22.4 The Atmosphere

- Recognise that the atmosphere is a mixture of gases that blanket the Earth.
- Evaluate how living organisms contribute to changes in our atmosphere.
- Appreciate that changes in atmospheric pressure affect weather.

Review 1: ● ● ● (/ /); Review 2: ● ● ● (/ /); Review 3: ● ● ● (/ /)

Chapter 23 The Interaction Between Earth and Space

23.1 The Earth and the Sun

- Demonstrate how shadows form.
- Compare day and night in terms of the spinning of the Earth.
- Use models to demonstrate and explain the seasons.

Review 1: ● ● ● (/ /); Review 2: ● ● ● (/ /); Review 3: ● ● ● (/ /)

23.2 The Earth and the Moon

- Outline the phases of the Moon.
- Describe how eclipses occur.
- Distinguish between solar and lunar eclipses.

Review 1: ● ● ● (/ /); Review 2: ● ● ● (/ /); Review 3: ● ● ● (/ /)

Chapter 24 Sources of Energy

24.1 Our Current Energy Needs

- Distinguish between renewable and non-renewable sources of energy.
- Outline how electricity is generated in a thermal power station.
- Describe the different types of renewable energy sources.

Review 1: ● ● ● (/ /); Review 2: ● ● ● (/ /); Review 3: ● ● ● (/ /)

24.2 Nuclear Energy

- Evaluate the global energy crisis.
- Distinguish between nuclear fission and fusion.

Review 1: ● ● ● (/ /); Review 2: ● ● ● (/ /); Review 3: ● ● ● (/ /)

24.3 Smart Technologies

- Consider future sources of renewable energy.

Review 1: ● ● ● (/ /); Review 2: ● ● ● (/ /); Review 3: ● ● ● (/ /)

Chapter 25 A Sustainable World

25.1 The Growth of the Human Population

- Recognise that humans are a relatively new species.
- Appreciate the significance of the huge explosion in the human population over the last 300 years.

Review 1: ● ● ● (/ /); Review 2: ● ● ● (/ /); Review 3: ● ● ● (/ /)

25.2 Human Impact on the Earth

- Describe human behaviours that damage the Earth.
- Consider pollution from agricultural, industrial and domestic sources.

Review 1: ● ● ● (/ /); Review 2: ● ● ● (/ /); Review 3: ● ● ● (/ /)

25.3 Meeting the Challenges Facing the Earth

- Analyse the challenges facing the Earth.
- Reflect on the importance of conserving the Earth's natural resources.
- Demonstrate an awareness that each person and every society must promote sustainability.

Review 1: ● ● ● (/ /); Review 2: ● ● ● (/ /); Review 3: ● ● ● (/ /)

Chapter 26 Space Travel

26.1 Space Flight

- Research the history of human space flight.
- Investigate how a rocket works.

Review 1: ● ● ● (/ /); Review 2: ● ● ● (/ /); Review 3: ● ● ● (/ /)

26.2 Looking at the Night Sky: Light Telescopes

- Distinguish between the types of light telescopes.
- Illustrate how light refracts through convex and concave lenses.

Review 1: ● ● ● (/ /); Review 2: ● ● ● (/ /); Review 3: ● ● ● (/ /)

26.3 Looking at the Night Sky: Radio Telescopes

- Describe the properties of waves.
- Consider the uses of radio telescopes.

Review 1: ● ● ● (/ /); Review 2: ● ● ● (/ /); Review 3: ● ● ● (/ /)

26.4 Space and the Future

- Distinguish between different types of space missions.

Review 1: ● ● ● (/ /); Review 2: ● ● ● (/ /); Review 3: ● ● ● (/ /)

Big Challenges

Big Challenge

Title: ....

Nature of Science	☐	Chapter number: ....
Biological World	☐	Page number: ....
Chemical World	☐	Date: ....
Physical World	☐	Lab partner(s): ....
Earth and Space	☐	....

1. What steps did you take to carry out this challenge?

2. Challenge review

a. What I enjoyed most about this challenge:

b. If I was to do this challenge again, I would do the following things differently:

c. I would like to extend this challenge in the following ways:

3. Key skills development

Key skills	How I developed these skills during this task

Big Challenge

Title: ....

Nature of Science	☐	Chapter number: ....
Biological World	☐	Page number: ....
Chemical World	☐	Date: ....
Physical World	☐	Lab partner(s): ....
Earth and Space	☐	....

1. What steps did you take to carry out this challenge?

2. Challenge review

a. What I enjoyed most about this challenge:

b. If I was to do this challenge again, I would do the following things differently:

c. I would like to extend this challenge in the following ways:

3. Key skills development

Key skills	**How I developed these skills during this task**

Big Challenge

Title: ....

Nature of Science ☐

Biological World ☐

Chemical World ☐

Physical World ☐

Earth and Space ☐

Chapter number: ....

Page number: ....

Date: ....

Lab partner(s): ....

....

1. What steps did you take to carry out this challenge?

2. Challenge review

a. What I enjoyed most about this challenge:

b. If I was to do this challenge again, I would do the following things differently:

c. I would like to extend this challenge in the following ways:

3. Key skills development

Key skills	How I developed these skills during this task

Big Challenge

Title:..

Nature of Science	☐	Chapter number: ....
Biological World	☐	Page number: ....
Chemical World	☐	Date:..
Physical World	☐	Lab partner(s):..
Earth and Space	☐	....

1. What steps did you take to carry out this challenge?

____

____

____

____

2. Challenge review

a. What I enjoyed most about this challenge:

____

____

b. If I was to do this challenge again, I would do the following things differently:

____

____

c. I would like to extend this challenge in the following ways:

____

____

3. Key skills development

Key skills	How I developed these skills during this task

Big Challenge

Title: ....

Nature of Science ☐

Biological World ☐

Chemical World ☐

Physical World ☐

Earth and Space ☐

Chapter number: ....

Page number: ....

Date: ....

Lab partner(s): ....

....

1. What steps did you take to carry out this challenge?

___

___

___

___

2. Challenge review

a. What I enjoyed most about this challenge:

___

___

b. If I was to do this challenge again, I would do the following things differently:

___

___

c. I would like to extend this challenge in the following ways:

___

___

3. Key skills development

Key skills	How I developed these skills during this task

Big Challenge

Title: ....

Nature of Science ☐

Biological World ☐

Chemical World ☐

Physical World ☐

Earth and Space ☐

Chapter number: ....

Page number: ....

Date: ....

Lab partner(s): ....

....

1. What steps did you take to carry out this challenge?

____

____

____

____

2. Challenge review

a. What I enjoyed most about this challenge:

____

____

b. If I was to do this challenge again, I would do the following things differently:

____

____

c. I would like to extend this challenge in the following ways:

____

____

3. Key skills development

Key skills	How I developed these skills during this task

Big Challenge

Title:..

Nature of Science ☐

Biological World ☐

Chemical World ☐

Physical World ☐

Earth and Space ☐

Chapter number: ....

Page number: ....

Date:..

Lab partner(s):...

....

1. What steps did you take to carry out this challenge?

2. Challenge review

a. What I enjoyed most about this challenge:

b. If I was to do this challenge again, I would do the following things differently:

c. I would like to extend this challenge in the following ways:

3. Key skills development

Key skills	**How I developed these skills during this task**

Big Challenge

Title: ....

Nature of Science	☐	Chapter number: ....
Biological World	☐	Page number: ....
Chemical World	☐	Date: ....
Physical World	☐	Lab partner(s): ....
Earth and Space	☐	....

1. What steps did you take to carry out this challenge?

____

____

____

____

2. Challenge review

a. What I enjoyed most about this challenge:

____

____

b. If I was to do this challenge again, I would do the following things differently:

____

____

c. I would like to extend this challenge in the following ways:

____

____

3. Key skills development

Key skills	How I developed these skills during this task

Big Challenge

Title: ....

Nature of Science ☐

Biological World ☐

Chemical World ☐

Physical World ☐

Earth and Space ☐

Chapter number: ....

Page number: ....

Date: ....

Lab partner(s): ....

....

1. What steps did you take to carry out this challenge?

____

____

____

____

2. Challenge review

a. What I enjoyed most about this challenge:

____

____

b. If I was to do this challenge again, I would do the following things differently:

____

____

c. I would like to extend this challenge in the following ways:

____

____

3. Key skills development

Key skills	How I developed these skills during this task

Big Challenge

Title: ....

Nature of Science	☐	Chapter number: ....
Biological World	☐	Page number: ....
Chemical World	☐	Date: ....
Physical World	☐	Lab partner(s): ....
Earth and Space	☐	....

1. What steps did you take to carry out this challenge?

2. Challenge review

a. What I enjoyed most about this challenge:

b. If I was to do this challenge again, I would do the following things differently:

c. I would like to extend this challenge in the following ways:

3. Key skills development

Key skills	How I developed these skills during this task